The Key to Selling Anybody: Once You Know It and Apply It Sales Will Take Off

Category: Business & Economics

Author: Bob Oros

Publisher: Bob Oros Publishing

ISBN: 978-1-387-19836-8

Copyright 2017

Description: How would you like to KNOW with absolute certainty that you could sell anybody? What if you had a magic key that would open the door to everyone you called on? You can! And once you know the secret formula - and apply it - your sales will take off!

Key words: sales techniques, motivating sales people, job in sales, sales manager training, sales course, manufacturing sales training, wholesale sales training, online sales training, distributor sales training, food sales jobs, food service sales, sales coaching,

ISBN 978-1-387-19836-8

90000

9 781387 198368

1. What is the key to selling anybody?

How would you like to KNOW with absolute certainty that you could sell anybody? What if you had a magic key that would open the door to everyone you called on? You can! And once you know the secret formula - and apply it - your sales will take off!

You will lose all feelings of call reluctance. Your confidence will double - or even triple. Your income will increase. You will have everything you ever wanted in life.

Here it is...

Find out by careful listening and questioning what your customer wants and let them know that you are sincerely interested in helping them get it.

Too simple? Let's try it on YOU. What do you want most in life. Do you want more cash? A new home? Money in the bank? Financial security?

Now, what if someone came into your life who was sincerely interested in helping you get those things? What if they went out of their way to show you how to increase your income? What if they helped you find ways to save and invest more of the money you work so hard to make so you could become financially secure? What if they helped you find and buy the home of your dreams? Would you want to know this person a little better?

On the other hand what if another person came into your life and all they wanted to do was sell you what THEY thought you should have? If they were overly aggressive, pushy, wanted to get you to do things you were not really interested in - how would you react? Do you see the difference? Wouldn't it feel good to have someone who is sincerely interested in helping you succeed?

I know what you are thinking - the only person who is that interested in ME is my mother! Remember, this is not about YOU - it is about selling - it is about your customer. Don't EXPECT anyone to be that interested in you. But that doesn't mean you cannot be that interested and helpful to your customers. This changes the whole focus.

Now I am going to show YOU how to make any amount of money you want by using this theory. You see, I AM interested in your success - I want you to sell more and make more money.

Let's say you want to make $120,000 over the next 12 months. Normally you would say to yourself - "THIS IS MY GOAL - I WILL MAKE $120,000 IN COMMISSIONS DURING THE NEXT 12 MONTHS." By taking this approach your focus is wrong.

Instead, try this... "I AM GOING TO GIVE $500 WORTH OF SERVICE EVERY DAY MONDAY THROUGH FRIDAY." Do you see the difference? Don't focus on the money - on what's in it for YOU - focus on GIVING THE SERVICE. The money will follow.

 This is the New definition of selling - service. This definition is so new it is not even in the dictionary or thesaurus. The dictionary says selling means to persuade, or influence to a course of action. The thesaurus says selling is "barter, exchange, trade, traffic, and vend. Nowhere does it say selling is SERVICE. Nowhere does it say selling is helping your customers become more successful and make more money.

 Let's put it another way. How much would someone PAY YOU to listen to your sales pitch. Zero - Right? Yet people pay thousands of dollars to consultants to ask questions - find out what they want - and help them get it. You can convey the same message to your customers. The true purpose of a consultative sales person is to find out what your customer wants and help them get it.

 To accomplish this you have to listen more that you talk. If you can get your customer to talk enough, they simply cannot disguise their real goals and real motives. They may try as hard as they can, but invariably they will "give themselves away". When they do - you have the key.

 YOU KNOW WHAT THEY WANT!

 Help them get it and you will have captured the true

meaning of being a sales professional.

A KNOWN DEMAND

In the mid-1800s, "A.T". Steward learned a valuable lesson that will help us all.

Here's what happened ...

As a young boy in Ireland, he saved up $1.50 and decided to try his hand at selling merchandise. He spent $0.87 (half of his money) on buttons and string. Then, he went door-to-door and tried to sell his goods.

The result? A total failure. Instead of giving up, he learned this valuable lesson, "I'll find out what the housewives really want and sell that." He did some research and discovered a "known demand."

Using the last of his money, he bought things that people really wanted. Because they wanted them, he had no difficulty at all in selling them for a profit. He said about this experience ... "I will never gamble again in business. I will first discover what people want."

A.T. moved to New York with some Irish-spun Belfast linens and laces (a known demand) and opened a shop on Broadway, A. T. Stewart & Co. From there he built the largest merchant business in the world focusing on his strengths and a known demand.

By 1848 he had built the largest retail store in the world at that time. Stewart also had branches of his company in different parts of the world and owned several mills and factories. Stewart had an annual income of $1,843,637 in 1863. His business success is estimated to have made him one of the twenty wealthiest people in history, with a fortune of approximately US$90 billion in 2012 prices.

How can we, as sales people, benefit from this story? Before you start to make your sales pitch, find out what your customer wants (a known demand) and help them get it. You won't have to sell, only help them buy.

All of my books and programs are based on what you, a person who sells for a living, want (a known demand).

Don't take my word for it...

Put these 3 words in Google: Bob Oros books

This is a great lesson. The more you become a consultant (I looked up the synonyms and love them) the more you will be of service to your customers. I think it is even necessary to change what we call ourselves. Words do have meaning and connotations. I think I prefer in this content, FSC, Food Service Consultant to DSR, District or Direct Sales Representative. You are what you call yourself. The more you hear "Service" and "Consultant" attached to who you are, the more you will believe it. And that is a very important first step.

James Ruth

 The consensus of salespeople is that we constantly have SELL, SELL, SELL on our minds, that is wrong. A successful salesperson has a listening mechanism like no other. Each and every time I visit my clients, do a sales call, or answer the phone I effectively listening to what they are saying. I take that feedback and when I go to service them I use what they have told me to provide them GREAT results. Our service is what we sell, not us!

Betsy Roberson

Time and time again I have walked out of a cold call with my sales manager and he has told me, "Take a step back and listen to what the customer was telling you." I was so focused on selling to the customer that I was not listening clearly.

 The customer was telling me the information I needed the entire time. I had another customer tell me his deli was heading down hill and he needed to do something to fix it. I made a suggestion of doing a little rearranging, he agreed.

I had one of our service technicians come out and help us move some equipment around his deli. The next day I went to follow up and see how he was doing and he had sold out of everything.

Jason Kirouac

One of my long term learning areas has been how to read between the lines of a customer's conversation and response to my questions. You have to be on the same wave length to interpret their meaning and resist focusing on your idea of what the customer needs. This takes a lot of practice and sharpening of your attention and listening skills. When I first started in sales, my sales manager and I made many calls together. After some of these meetings he would surprise me by saying something the customer got across to him that I did not even hear in the conversation.

Crocker Smith

Yesterday I made the conscience decision that I would no longer ask a prospect the following question in this environment: "How's business?" That can lead to a question you don't know the answer to and take you down a road that's very difficult to turn around the beer truck on (if you know what I mean). Instead I asked the following question. "Have you discussed your goals over the next six months or year with your current provider? I ask because if you don't mind telling me as well I'd like to hear them too. I just might be able to help, or, point you in the direction of someone who has a different expertise than mine that might be able to help you". After having this conversation with a prospect yesterday I was fortunate enough to land a meeting with a prominent vineyard next Friday.

Michael S. Hutchison

Thinking of selling as service makes me feel far more comfortable in a sales position. It is easier to approach people with the intention of helping them, or being of service to them. People are always looking for ways to reach their goals and I think this approach will ensure success. If I can serve others by helping them reach their goals, and simultaneously make a sale, it's a win-win situation.

Tiffany Kish

I think it's having the ability to ask the right questions and really listen to the answers. Have you every had someone ask how you were doing and you learn thru body language that it was just a question and they could really care less how you are doing? One of my mentors shared with me something that has stuck with me. We were coming up with a game plan for one particular client and I wasn't prepared to take notes. He asked me how confident do you feel when you are at a restaurant and the waitress comes to your table of 10 to take your order and she isn't writing down what's being ordered. The order is bound to be messed up and that can happen in any situation if you aren't listening and taking notes.

Becky Akins

When people see a sales person coming, usually their first reaction is to go the other way. In their mind, they know the sales person is just there to sell them something whether they need it or not. To over come this, you need to listen to the client and find out their needs. Then make a suggestion that will help solve their issue. Once, you show how you can relieve their problem then you are able to start establishing a relationship & sell the service you offer. If you don't have the solution to their problem, then be up front & honest with them. Never try to sell them something they don't need or it will come back to haunt you in the future. Being a consultant is the first step to the real sale.

Carla McCrea

This is a great way to think of selling. It makes sense when you think about it. If we go in to a company to "sell" something we are already hurting ourselves. The people we are talking to each and every day hear the same pitch and already have a scripted answer for us. If we go in and find out what they need we take ourselves out of the salesperson mode and into a consulting mode. This allows us to adapt our "pitch" to give them exactly what they need. We offer more services than what most businesses think we do, and by consulting we can offer everything.

Brandon Sanchez

2. How can you separate yourself from your competition?

Give me one good reason why I should buy from you!

I get sales people calling me all the time. You all look alike - sound alike - make the same promises, what makes you any different?

You have to separate yourself from the competition. You have to be different. You have to be better.

One of the best ways to separate yourself from the competition is to know everything there is to know about your products and services. If you know what you are talking about, the customer feels it and starts trusting what you say.

The goal is not necessarily to be able to give very technical characteristics. The goal is to know the product so much in depth that you are able to simplify the complicated characteristics into powerful advantages for the client to use the product. This means applying what you learn by turning your product knowledge into benefits and presenting these benefits to your customers.

Attend all the presentations, seminars, courses and talks by renowned speakers that are available. Don't consider these an expense, but an investment to better yourself.

You will always learn from these presentations, seminars,

courses and talks. Accept all supplier invitations for sales, marketing or product information seminars.

When you have the opportunity to attend an industry convention or regional training function talk to people who are more successful than you are and learn everything you can from them.

After a while, from all the information you store in your mind from all these different sources, you develop your own style and your own recipes for success that work best for you.   This is the unique strategy that will keep you one step ahead of your competition.

Learning and self-improvement implies one essential feeling: the desire to be better, the desire to improve.

Many sales people are often surprised to find themselves dropping behind their competitors, but when they examine themselves, they find that they have stopped growing because they have ceased their effort to keep up with new selling techniques, new products and new marketing strategies.

Some people are so busy trying to learn the "tricks of the trade", they never learn the trade. Your ability as a sales person is always on the move, either one way or the other. It is either getting better or getting worse. Everything you do not use is slipping away.

Some sales people complain about having to attend sales meetings or training seminars. Even if they knew everything offered by a training program, they still need the training. The essence of successful training is to build confidence by helping to improve the skills you already have.

Seminars and sales meetings are a great place to start, however, it is ultimately up to you to improve your skills. The person who continuously looks for new ideas and better methods of selling is the one who moves forward.

Commit to spending time every day learning more about your business. One hour a day spent studying your business will make you one of the top international experts in your field in 5 years.

One of the most successful sales people I know is a manufacturers rep for a seafood company. I first met him at a trade show where I asked him a question about a specific species of fish. He reached in his brief case and pulled out a 3 ring binder that was about 3 inches thick. This binder was filled with magazine articles, pictures, charts, newspaper clippings and notes that he had collected. He was continuously collecting information about his specialty. He was one of the most well informed sales people I have ever met, and is it any wonder he was so successful?

What are you doing to improve your knowledge and separate yourself from your competitor? I once looked at all the books on selling I had on my shelf and thought about how much useful information is in them yet going unused. I decided to do something bold. I took the books one by one and cut out all the things I wanted to learn and apply. I pasted the information on 3 x 5 cards and organized them by topic. I began reviewing them every day until I knew them and experienced what I had learned. Once you know something and then you do it with a conscious effort, you will really know it. This was done 25 years ago and I still have the 3 x 5 cards today. Many of the concepts are spread throughout this course. Today, whenever I buy a book I buy two. One to keep and one to cut up.

It doesn't mater what system you use for increasing your knowledge bank, the important thing is that you learn and apply something new every day. A good place to start is by reading, absorbing and APPLYING the course you are now taking. As we previously discussed, APPLICATION is the key.

People have asked why they should buy from me and I tell them it is because I am the best at what I do, period. No one will do the work that I will to get the answers they need. I am better than the next guy because I truly care about them as a business partner. If they will allow me to work with them I will do everything in my power to help their business grow and prosper. I tell prospects that they are long term investments for me. I will put in the work and do the research that is necessary that they don't have time to do in order to help them grow. Even if that means that I have to suggest product that I don't handle. By putting their needs and concerns first, it shows the customer that I am truly committed to their bottom line. This might not put dollars in my pocket on that particular item but it solidifies the relationship with the customer even further. Once they see that my strategy isn't about a quick sale I become the guy they call first.

Dave Ferren

There's just something different about a conversation with someone when you know and understand the topic. I don't care if it is sports or current events. When you have knowledge about a topic you handle yourself differently. You exude confidence. You listen better. The same applies to selling your product. When a customer senses your expertise, the conversation changes from "what is he trying to sell me?" to "I know he can help."

Jim Ruth

I've always been amazed when I've delt with salesman who had no product knowledge of what they are selling. I've had this happen so often with car salesman that I can't even count how many times.

One of the most amusing things [to me] was when I was looking a large high power audio amplifier at a chain electronics store. It had a THX certification on it. The salesman took it upon himself to tell me what THX was and told me that George Lucas had invented it [seems he had never even read the brochure on this amplifier or any other piece of gear that was THX certified].

 I was about doubled over laughing about his description and he couldn't understand why. I then explained to him that George Lucas was a movie producer and not an engineer and that Lucas Films endorses THX. I did kindly tell him what THX stood for. I then asked him what kind of output devices the amplifier used and got the deer-in-the – headlights look. He had no real knowledge at all about what he was trying to sell other than it was the most expensive stuff in the store. It's important to know everything you can about the products you are selling because you will find the customer going somewhere else.

Cary McAfee

A customer who is an expert in his field can spot a novice salesperson almost immediately. I have had questions thrown at me just to test my knowledge. If the person you are trying to sell to is way ahead of you, they will not put much value on your ability to help them succeed.

Crocker Smith

I was one of those "tricks of the trade" sales people. That's one of the reasons I signed up for this course. Very quickly you find that truly asking questions of your customer is the best knowledge you can gain. And since people generally love to speak about themselves you can sit and get volumes of information just asking some simple questions. Then if you truly are a student of your profession you start to gain the knowledge to be successful beyond your wildest dreams. Every time I sign on a new customer I ask them why they decided to do business with me. I take that and write it down in the "book of successes". I learn form each one of those.

Michael S. Hutchison

If you are truly interested in the product you are selling then learning everything about it would be a very smooth process. Learning every aspect of the product is the key to success. I would not want to purchase something from someone that is unsure of what they are selling me. Selling something that you are not familiar with could really hurt the business also because if someone is mislead about something they purchased they would hold it against the company as well as the salesperson.

Jamie R. Friend

Concern and Enthusiasm I believe are the two best ways to separate you from the rest of the pack.

1st Concern- Show your client you want to help SOLVE their problems (not add to them). Remember you are in this together. Ask your client what the biggest obstacle they are facing right now. Key here is to be quite and listen. What if their problem has nothing to do with you? IT DOSE NOT MATTER. Hopefully you have researched the industry and talked with others in the industry. Share some helpful hints or ideas. When those issues are out of the way- the customer is VERY willing to talk about how you can now help solve other issues that DO involve you.

2nd Enthusiasm- Show your client you are happy to see or talk with them. Never let them see you sweat. Smile, Smile, Smile- use inflection in your voice. They are NOT just another stop or call on your route- You are truly happy to talk with them. If you're not talking with them- someone else is.

Be Sharp & Shinny:

Like any piece of fine silver- we tarnish over time. Researching, reading and learning new ideas or refreshing old ones will polish our inner Silver to a Shine. This will set you apart from other dull knives in the drawer.

Keeping it Simple,

Teresa Cloninger

Knowing and applying the things you learn will separate you from your competition. Knowing your product will give you the edge needed to get the account your competitor did not. Don't feed them a line if you don't know what you're talking about. And be ready to back up your promises. To become a successful sales person you must continue to learn. remember to know your product in depth but don't overwhelm your client with things that they don't need to know.

Brian Spraggins

3. What is the best way to build a personal relationship?

What has caused you, in the past, to think about the possibility of doing something besides selling? Here is the answer. The indifferent, reluctant, defensive attitude that greets you every time you make a sales call is what defeats nearly everyone who fails in a selling career.

Wouldn't it be nice if you were welcomed everywhere you went? If potential customers said "yes, come in, tell me more?"

What can you do or say that will make a prospect treat you favorably? How can you get them to change from indifference and reluctance to being receptive and looking at your products and services?

Here is the answer. Changing their attitude starts by controlling your attitude. You have to continue to feel good about them even if they don't feel good about you, or themselves.

Not as easy as it sounds. Keep in mind that you are not selling products and services, you are selling yourself.

If your company comes out with a new product you can be sure every competitor is finding out how it can be duplicated. The same goes for services. Come out with a new way of providing extra services and you will have an edge for a while. However, it won't be long before a competitor will be offering the same service.

Adding extra services without increasing your price is actually lowering your gross profit. As one president of a large distribution company said, "All I really have is a warehouse full of commodities."

If the difference is the personal relationship you can establish with your customers, what can you do to enhance that relationship? To answer this question all you have to do is ask what makes you like or dislike someone you are doing business with?

You like people who like you. Someone who is interested in all aspects of your business. Someone who talks about the things you want and the goals you are trying to accomplish.

Here is the secret of getting past their indifference. Here is what would make YOU buy from someone. When someone has the tools to help you succeed and their main purpose is to provide those tools for your use and help you achieve your goals, it is impossible not to feel the desire to work with them.

Let's say that again... it is important.

When someone has the tools to help YOU succeed and their main purpose is to provide those tools for YOUR use and help YOU achieve YOUR goals, it is IMPOSSIBLE not to feel the desire to work with them.

Most of the time customers and prospects don't know what they want. You, as a sales consultant, have to help your customers identify their goals and show them you are interested in helping them succeed.

Sounds altruistic, I know. But consider this - as one very successful sales person put it when asked why he did so much for his customers, why he always went the extra mile and always put his customers first; "because I am a very selfish person. I like to make money."

Another benefit of this "altruistic" approach - it gets your mind off of yourself and you lose your fear.

I have to admit this is the area I have had the most trouble with. It has always been hard for me to get over the awkwardness of meeting people the first time and developing a relationship. Probably why I have spent so many years doing technical work behind the scenes. They need my technical expertise to solve their problems and get them up and running again. Machines can be quite complex but I can fix them and they don't judge you.

The years I spent as a horsemanship instructor probably helped me as much as anything in developing relationships. I know people were coming to me to learn how to ride a horse or improve their skills but I was able to develop a program for getting my message across and making them feel comfortable. I try to carry some of those principles over into my work these days.

1. I first find out what their goals are. I ask them what they have done in the past and where they would like to go.

2. I convey to them that I am interested in them as individuals. I have a liberal neighbor who tries to put everybody into groups [I found out that is part of liberal thinking]. Bugs the hell out of him that I am not of that mindset.

3. I always end a session on a positive note when possible. That way they are looking forward to seeing me again.

Of course I used these as horse program director for several years. What made it easier was that people were coming to me. I have had to work at it more when I've been calling on customers. The intial breaking the ice seems to be the hardest for me calling on people. Once I get to know them a little bit it gets easier.

Cary McAfee

Once you gain their confidence and trust you are no longer a waste of time, a threat, an adversary – you are a problem solver, a profit enabler and a friend. This is one of the ways that I judge my personal success.

Crocker Smith

I just had the conversation with a prospect today that really didn't want to speak with me until I said the following. "Kim if I understand you correctly what you're saying is that value is more important than price. Is that correct? Then you'll be happy to know that I'm not going to give you a price until we exhausted a plausible match to every product you have in the building. And I'll do this for one simple reason: If I come in here with a clip board full of prices and an order guide and I don't ask you where you've been and where you want to go I'm like every other salesperson that knocks on your door - and I don't think that's good for your business. Would you agree?" She asked me to come back next week so we could discuss her menu and start to do cuttings at a weekly predetermined time. She gave me a copy of her menu so we could talk about it next week. Nice conversation and I believe I sold myself to her in the five minutes I had to set up another appointment.

Michael S. Hutchison

It always seems there is nothing more people hate than sales people coming by and just giving their pitch because they have to, not because they want to. When you get your turn down comments it's your job to understand, look at why they are not interested and build on that - not recite a script in your head of what you are suppose to say next if the customer says no.

To me this is hugely important. It's like collections. If I call just giving a script and don't give any understanding or make them feel like I am listening to their situation. The longer it will take me to get paid.

Nisan Krawetz

Being honest and friendly with customers will gain their trust in you to ensure that they want to do business with you. You must show the customer that you are truly interested in helping them. I personally would not only want to succeed, but to honestly want to help people. If I help someone accomplish something and know that they are happy with me this would make me feel very successful.

Jamie R. Friend

"Treat others as you would like to be treated." This is

probably something your Mother has told you many times as a child. I feel that acknowledging the importance of your clients needs and showing that you value their time, will show them that you are there looking out for their best interests. This feeling of a valued relationship will create a long lasting business relationship that they will share with others.

Tonya Sauer

I worked for Baskin Robbins for a number of years. Irv Robbins personal stationary was printed with the saying on the bottom " If people were not different, all we would make is Vanilla." A great portion of that companies success is that they were focused on their customer, not what was convenient for production or distribution.

 We certainly have more efficient means to take an order, direct data entry, answering machines, fax machines...I hate them as a customer, and I hate them as a sales CONSULTANT, they leave out the most important thing, the personal perspective that will allow me to help the customer achieve their goals.

Mark Brockett

Altruism, to be honest I have never used the word but so true. If a client believes that you attain the attitude to act for his benefit, a strong, trusting relationship will develop. When a client senses that you are there to help him control costs and not cost him money by offering your services, he trusts that you have the best interest in mind for his business. A friendship has now developed and he will tell his other friends thus creating a pyramid effect.

Gregg Nixon

4. Why do you lose business?

What is the easiest way for a competitor to take a customer away from you? Why do you lose accounts to your competitors?

Here are some reasons that sound good: Our service isn't up to par. Our prices are too high. We have too many out-of-stocks. My competitor is better known in my market.

I have a surprise for you. When you lose an account it is mostly due to one reason. I would say that 95% of all the accounts you lose to a competitor are for this single reason! This single reason will enable you to take away more business from your competitor than you can handle.

It's easier than you think. Here's why. Your competitors are taking their customers for granted. I guarantee it! Let me say that again in capital letters...

YOUR COMPETITORS ARE TAKING THEIR CUSTOMERS FOR GRANTED.

And do you know what else? So are you - I know, I know - you don't want to hear that. It's true - you know it and I know it.

Lets put it to the test. Do you feel appreciated? Probably not. Would you like a little appreciation? If your answer is yes - you are not alone. In a recent survey 6,600 people were asked two questions:

1. Do you receive as much praise, recognition and appreciation as you feel you deserve?

6,415 SAID NO

2. Would you perform your job better if you were given more praise, recognition and appreciation?

6,495 SAID YES

This, of course, doesn't apply to you - you are in sales - it is up to you to GIVE appreciation not GET it. The point is - most people feel unappreciated.

Here's more proof - a real life example: I was helping a small foodservice distributor look for a way to promote their business. We thought about a food show, however, due to the small size of the company we felt that it would be too big of an undertaking. After a lot of talking we finally came up with a program we called a "customer appreciation dinner."

We contacted 20 of his suppliers and asked them to participate by serving dinner to the customers and at the same giving them the opportunity to show samples of their products. All the suppliers agreed and we put together a buffet line concept with the theme being that we want to show our customers that we appreciate their business.

We decided to use an RSVP format so we would know how many people would show up, and we could tell the suppliers how many people they could plan on feeding. We arranged to have the dinner at a Holiday Inn with a room large enough to hold 108 people at one time.

We sent out 525 invitations expecting to get about 200 RSVP's. The invitation said, "When was the last time someone took you to dinner to show you how much they appreciate your business?"

Not knowing the power of our theme, "Customer Appreciation Dinner", we had 525 RSVP's! We had to turn the tables FIVE TIMES during the evening. Every restaurant in the small southern town was closed with a sign on the door saying "Closed - we went out for dinner."

The normal procedure is to get an account, wine and dine them during the honeymoon period, and then put them on auto pilot. You are guilty of it, aren't you? Admit it.

How can you take away business from a competitor? Here's the secret. Get a small order from your competitor's customer and then show that you REALLY appreciate their business. Too simple? - You WILL stand out and be noticed.

Sure, you gave the customer a discount - THEY should appreciate YOU! Your customer is the one who writes out those big checks every week - they are not thinking about how much they appreciate the small discount they got -

they are wondering if YOU appreciate the amount of business THEY are giving YOU.

Your customers pay your mortgage, put your kids through school, make your car payments, pay for your retirement plan. Your top twenty customers - Do you thank them enough? Do you show them that you appreciate their business? More than likely the answer is no.

Give your customers the attention and appreciation they are hungry for. Give your prospects the attention and appreciation they are not getting from their current supplier and you will take away the business.

Few things are more gratifying than gratitude, and very few sales people express their gratitude as much as they should.

Appreciation can go a lot farther than just saying thank you. How many thank you notes did you send last year? Your competitors are not doing it. It's the little messages of gratitude that will make a big difference.

I was sitting in a buyer's office when a fax came in for him. He seemed a little upset so I asked him if there was anything wrong. He said a salesman had just left with a large order and he just faxed a thank you note.

I thought that was pretty good for a sales person to take the time to send a thank you fax. However, the buyer said he was going to cancel the order, but because of the thank you note it became too difficult to call and cancel.

You never know what insurance your thank you notes, follow up phone calls and extra attention is providing. Here is more proof.

Headquarters wanted to know why a small pizza shop was performing way beyond everyone's expectations. They were number one in a large national chain – yet located in a small town with a lot of competition. When they investigated they found that before closing they would go through their deliveries and call everyone to make sure their pizza was good!

CAN YOU IMAGINE THAT? A thank you call from a PIZZA SHOP?

I just bought a new house. After the closing I never heard a peep from the broker - nothing - zero! I even had to call his office and tell them to come and get their sign out of my yard!

No - Service is not the reason you lose business.

No - Price is not the reason you lose business.

No - Your competitor's image in the market is not the reason.

No - it's none of those things.

The reason you lose, on average TWENTY-FIVE PERCENT OF YOUR BUSINESS EVERY YEAR is because you didn't listen to your mother when she told you to say "Thank You."

I always make an effort to show my small customers the same gratitude and appreciation as I do my larger accounts. I was in the Restaurant business working for a large corporation where I purchased over $300,000 yearly. Later I went to my own small business of $80,000. I noticed how differently I was treated by some of the people at my supplier and always remember how offended that made me feel.

Marion Blomeke

I think that we become complacent far too easy. We feel like we are owed the business after we put in a little time. We forget that it is an ongoing experience and that we have to continue to nurture our clients to help them grow their business as well as ours.

Tammy McReynolds

I recently lost a large account, partly because of low-balling by a competitor, but partly because I probably did not give them the attention they deserved. It was not intentional, it just happened. My other customers are benefiting by my mistake because of my increased attention and appreciation of their business. I will never lose another account because of my taking them for granted.

Larry Edmondson

I have recently picked up two accounts that had heard of our company from other customers of ours. I was told by both owners that they wanted to go with our company because of the continued support and appreciation the other salesmen have shown the other customers in the community. It has proven to me that a little extra time and effort, shown to not only a customers business but the client themselves, goes along way. Ill start today by saying thank you to John and Tommy, you have been a big help in the starting of my career.

Jason Kirouac

One of my most enjoyable sales was continually calling on a customer who never gave me any business. He was satisfied with my competitor until he slacked off on his calls to this customer. I will never forget watching this customer sign my order pad and thinking about my competitor driving around not even knowing he had lost a big sale. I think he found out two weeks later.

Crocker Smith

In the past year I was able to gain business from the competitor just by showing up! They had gone months without seeing their sales rep, and it was an easy sale for me. However, I am working harder to make sure my customers know how much I appreciate them so I am not put in the situation that the competitor takes the business from me. I see my accounts on the same day and same time every week. If for some reason I am running late of off, I always make sure I notify the customer.

Candy Swift

I called a prospective client the other day asking if I could simply stop by and introduce myself. He mentioned to me that he has been doing business with one particular company for years. I went on to ask questions about the service he's been receiving from them and that's when he said " it's been months since I've seen them."

Talk about being taken advantage of.... This was a true example of him not feeling appreciated. I simply said that I understand and respect the loyality you have with your current provider but options are good. He invited to stop by anytime I was in the area. I know for certain that if I continue to stop in and call to check on his needs he will give us the opportunity.

Becky Akins

I recently experienced taking a customer for granted but from the favorable side of the fence. I visited a new customer last week to thank him for his business. During the conversation, he told me the salesperson from the staffing agency he normally uses had not contacted a single time him in 3 months. He contemplated calling the agency to place the recent order but gave me the opportunity instead since I have been keeping in touch with him on a monthly basis. He even informed me my rate was higher but has appreciated the service and the quality of the employees we have delivered so far. SO FAR is the reminder for me to continuously thank our customers for their business.

Gregg Nixon

I love to thank my clients past, present and future. I send out thank you cards that I ordered specifically to do so. With sayings such as "thank you for your continued loyal patronage", "your confidence helps us rise to new heights, thank you for your business" and "just to let you know, we appreciate your business". I like to take candy to them on a regular basis and I take them birthday gifts if I know when their birthday is. I find it a joy to go the extra mile and I consider each and every one of them #1 whether I have 1 employee with them or 100. If it weren't for them, I wouldn't be where I am today. And I love it!!

Kathie Luttrell

Ten years ago, I set a goal for myself to say thank you. I had a very successful restaurant and the best staff I ever had. During one of our quarterly staff meetings I gave a simple form to each staff member to critique each of the salaried managers.

I was shocked to learn that I did not say "thank you" or "good job" enough. The staff gave me high marks and really enjoyed working for me but this was the reoccurring theme in the comment section. I can tell you from that moment on, I try much harder to say thank you. I will never achieve my goal of saying thank you enough. You can never reach that goal.

I call customers on a periodic basis to see how things are going and thank them for their business. I tell them the purpose of the call was just to say thank you for the business and just to see if I can be of help. It goes a long way.

Rolland DeGregorio

WOW!! This lesson was very good. And it made me think how HUGE the words Thank You can be when they are said over and over. The example about everyone sending back an RSVP was powerful. This lesson made me stop and think "What can I do to always say "thank you", even after I leave the customer. I plan on adding to my schedule a weekly time to send out a thank you card to each new contact I have made for the week. I routinely stop in to say thank you to my current customers and to customers who have used us in the past. I know how good it would make me feel if I got a thank you card for listening just because someone stopped by to tell me about their services and I took the time to listen. I always want my customers to feel that I am genuine and looking out for their best interests. I wouldn't want to be taken for granted and I would never want to give that impression to any of my customers.

Patsy Clements

Thank you does go a long way. It shouldn't just be said to the external customers though, it should be to the internal customers as well that help and support you in achieving the sale. None of us could sell products on our own, or bring in product necessary to service a new account - it's the whole team that you have in the office working for you, as well as the customer that came on board. Sometimes it's so easy to lose sight of saying "thank you" since you just assume that the other parties involved know that you are thankful. This has given me the motivation to call up my customers, just to see how things are going, and to thank them for their business!

Jo Welch

5. How do you handle rejection?

You are probably being asked to make more sales calls and you are having a problem. Here's why:

More calls = more rejection.

Before I give you my technique for handling rejection let me share with you a comment I received some time ago when I published the following information in a magazine article.

"I just read your article, Handling Rejection - Understand Why. Wow! I started my new business a couple of months ago. I refined my business plan, got leads, did a direct mailing, then I was frozen at the follow up call. I didn't have cold calling, or follow up call experience. Your article describes exactly how I feel and it has given me the confidence to act like I now have the right to place that call. Thank you for writing it. I really enjoyed it. And you probably made me lots of money because now I'm going to make my calls."

The reason the comment is so important is to let you know that you are not alone. Everybody in sales gets that FEELING. You know the one I'm talking about. If you don't it's only because you haven't been in sales long enough to make your first call. You are still under the delusion that everyone wants to see you and buy from you.

Here is the biggest reason you don't make the call in the first place:

You are worried about what they will think of you if you are unable to answer a tough question they might ask, or overcome an objection?

Here's a secret - they don't think about you.

Most people spend 98% of their time thinking about themselves. In the 2% of time left over there is not much room to squeeze you in.

It has always been amazing to me how some people can let negative thoughts or comments occupy so much space in their mind. Some people let these thoughts freeze their activities and kill their career in sales. Every thought you carry around and dwell on should be paying rent for taking up space in your mind!

I am always impressed with people who have conquered their fear of rejection. I am much more impressed with them then I am the people who happen to stumble onto a big sale. I am always looking for them because I am so eager to learn how they do it.

Here's an example and a good lesson in rejection.

My wife and I were in the kitchen and noticed two young gentlemen with white shirts and black ties approaching our front door. My wife said YOU get the door.

I really enjoy talking with people so I greeted the visitors eager to ask them some questions. The two young men were of a certain religious faith on a mission. During the conversation I asked them how many doors they had to knock on before someone invited them in. They said on a good day ONE OUT OF FIFTY will talk to us! Think of it - FORTY NINE PEOPLE TURNED THEM DOWN BEFORE ONE WOULD TALK TO THEM. I asked them how they handled the 49 who rejected them and here is what they told me: "We pray for them!"

Now there's a plan! Instead of letting them upset you why not just say to yourself - "That dummy has such a closed mind he won't even listen to me and with that kind of an attitude his business will probably go belly up because of his lack of interest in anything new! Since I don't see his name on the bail-out list I'd better send up a prayer for him because he is going to need more help then I can possibly give him anyway!!"

What just happened? YOU rejected HIM!

And THERE LIES THE KEY TO YOUR SUCCESS.

If your closing ratio for opening new customers is 1 out of every 10 here is what you have to do: Line up 10 calls with the idea that 9 will tell you to get lost! Nine of them are going to try to humiliate you. Nine of them are going to try and make you fail.

It's really a good thing for us in sales that there are a lot of dumb bunnies out there anyway.

Why?

Because they help the sales profession from becoming overcrowded. Let the other professions lock themselves in an office from 8 to 5 and quiver every time the boss walks by. Let the willy-nilly wimps take care of all those mundane activities. Let the timid non assertive people who wake up every day in fear of their job hope and pray there is someone out there who knows how to CREATE BUSINESS. WHO KNOWS THAT BEING REJECTED IS PART OF THE GAME.

It takes "GUTS" to be in sales.

I looked the word "guts" up in the thesaurus - here's what came back - courage, dauntlessness, heart, mettle, moxie, pluck, resolution, spirit, backbone, grit, intestinal fortitude, nerve, spunk! Put THAT list next to the phone or on the dash board because THAT DESCRIBES YOU!

When somebody rejects you just say this:

"Two words for you buddy - thank you!" You are simply that much closer to finding a REAL customer.

The bigger the stakes, the bigger the chance for rejection. If you were playing in the Super Bowl and your team lost because YOU fumbled the ball, THAT would be the ultimate rejection. How many millions of people would be rejecting you? Without taking that risk of rejection you lose before you even start. You will never be in the Super Bowl of Sales.

Nobody likes rejection. It's natural to feel some disappointment when you hear someone say "no."

The issue is how you deal with that rejection. When you hear no it means you are doing your job.

The issue of rejection is not what the prospect or customer thinks of you, but what you think of yourself. Another important part of dealing with rejection is understanding why they rejected you.

Here is what I mean.

The reason may have to do with timing - at this particular moment in time, as you are making your sales call, they may be perfectly happy with their current vendor. They may have just had a fight with their spouse and you happen to be the first one they talk to. They may have not had anything to eat all day and it is affecting their mood. They may have just been turned down for a promotion - or a loan - or a new job. They may have just had to fire one of their employees. All these things have nothing to do with you.

You have to train your mind to respond to rejection with enthusiasm.

I sold insurance many years ago and part of the training program was to go into a small office and make 10 cold phone calls. The phone was wired with speakers so the rest of the trainees could sit in the adjoining room and listen to the conversations. After you made your phone calls you would be critiqued by your colleagues. That was easy.

The hard part is when you are by yourself sitting in your car waiting for your appointment time, or when you are sitting alone at your desk in your home office and have to make the call. THAT is when is strikes.

A friend told me about a company where he applied for a job. The company sold something OTHER than vacuum cleaners. They sold computers. Yet, as part of his job qualification program he had to sit in a room with a telephone and phone book, call 100 people at random and try to get an appointment to do a vacuum cleaner demonstration. Over half of the applicants would quit before they made it to 50 calls.

This fear of rejection could be costing you a lot of money if you are not making calls because of it.

How do you overcome this fear of approaching someone? Here's what you have to do even if you don't feel like it - you have to ask.

The bottom line of selling is to ask for your customer's or prospect's business. Don't be afraid to do just that. Don't be embarrassed to ask for what you want. Don't fear rejection. Don't worry about making the customer angry. Don't be immobilized by your own timidity. Don't have negative thoughts that will set you up for failure.

Instead say to yourself... "I love what I do - I love to sell. I am in the right place at the right time. I have nothing to lose and everything to gain by making the call and asking for the business."

Selling is really simple. Selling is asking enough people to buy your products and services. Selling is weeding out all the one's that don't "get it." All you have to do is ask enough people to buy your products and services and SOMEONE WILL BUY! If you don't make the request the customer is already ahead - you've made things easy for them! You've eliminated the possibility that they might actually say yes.

Don't let fear of rejection keep you from making the call. Approach each prospect with the idea that you are qualifying THEM. Do they qualify to buy from ME? Do they have the means to pay for what I'm selling? Are they smart enough to realize the value of what I am offering? Are they worth the investment of my valuable time? Is there enough business on the table for me to spend time and money to get my share?

When calling on a new prospect those are the questions

you want answered. When you make a prospect call or a cold call, there is always a certain amount of hesitation because the pressure is on YOU to make a presentation. Forget about making a presentation. Go in with the attitude that you are QUALIFYING THEM. If they don't measure up THEY are the poor souls that miss out! They are the ones that lose.

Read this next sentence carefully. To reduce call hesitation when calling on a prospect, make the call with the idea that you are qualifying the prospect and you can reject THEM if they don't measure up.

Now you have the power. You have the power of rejection. You don't like to be rejected. So why give anyone the power to reject you? You are simply making the call to INVESTIGATE. You are there to get the FACTS ABOUT THEM. What you have to sell may be way beyond their understanding. It may be way over their head. To find out, you have to make the call and do the interview.

There is a certain fear you feel when trying to sell something to a stranger. But now you are not trying to sell on that initial contact.

You are eliminating unqualified prospects.

Of course, if you make the call and find that they are qualified and eager to do business with you - take the order. But don't let fear of rejection keep you from walking through the door and looking them in the eye.

Don't let fear of rejection keep you from picking up the phone and making the call. You - your products - your services - are the answer to their prayers.

Are they good enough to do business with YOU!

The reason people aim too low and expect to fail is they don't know how to handle the success when it comes and they don't want to go through the pain of rejection. If you don't expect to do great things there is no failure. With no failure comes no pain of rejection if it doesn't happen. The hardest thing about expecting to do great things is when all of your efforts result in brutal rejection.

Dave Ferren

I have to admit that the fear of rejection is the biggest problem I have dealt with most of my life. As I have gotten older it has gotten easier but I still have to work at it.

At one time in my life in the late 70's it was so bad it was hindering me from doing almost anything. I had gotten laid off from a company and was still trying to sort it all out without realizing it wasn't my fault. I can even remember searching for another job, even getting as far as the parking lot and than just driving on by because I did not want to be rejected again in the interview.

I eventually realized that it wasn't me and that most of the people who said no were not worth of my time. I have a lot of talent and can help almost anybody. I just have to remind myself of that sometimes.

Cary McAfee

Prior to becoming a Naval Recruiter you attend a 5 week sales course with 25-30 new people you never met before and 5 instructors there to help you succeed or fail. The first thing they do is put in your mind what it takes to put 1 person in the service. You have to get three people to pass the physical, in order to pass the physical you have to get 5 people to pass the aptitude test, you need 8 appointments and to get the 8 appointments you have to make twelve calls. They tell you this the first hour of your first day. Next they tell you a cold call is always an interruption, if you get rejected say thank you for your time and mark down on a piece of paper 1. Only 11 more calls and I'll have my 8 appts.

Ralph Scalici

I think a great thing to remember is that no matter whom you are calling on, no matter what position they hold, no matter how big the business, no matter how large the office, no matter how many employees, they are just people like you and me! We all put our shoes on the same way every morning, one at a time!

Lynn Mosely

What a great lesson! It reminds me that as much as people dislike sales people, people rely heavily on us to make informed decisions constantly. People do want to buy just not be SOLD. Everyone on this planet is a salesman/saleswoman at some point. Weather its talking about this great new movie that just came out or the hottest gadget on the market. When you reccommend these products to your friends you don't disown them because they didn't take your advice. So why get upset if a customer doesn't choose you and your company to do business with. The only way to kill a NO is to keep going until you get a YES and you forget about all the NO's you got. The reason I LOVE sales is not because of selling, it's because some of the richest people in the world will tell you that you must learn to sell if you want the financial rewards that will set you free. That's why I personaly choose sales, to learn how to sale better then anyone else I know. Life is one big game, have fun. The truth is, don't take life to serious cause no one gets out alive.

Dwayne Mitchell

Probably one of the hardest areas I have had to constantly battle with is peoples perception of sales people. The first time I realized a customers viewed me as a "used cars salesperson" I was honestly devastated. I have prided myself over the years on a solid work ethic along with my integrity and character so imagine when I realized that a percentage of my customers automatically assume I was out to " take advantage of them".

 Your course has helped me to realize not to take it personally and that it is okay (more than okay, it is expected) for me to make a living and there are many ways (and yes, some creative) to do that. I have realized that I deserve to get paid when I have serviced a customer and that sometimes it has been me falling for their game!

 I still get a little shocked when a customer makes a comment about my pricing or other service but I have also learned that in many ways it is a dance and the question is, who is leading? Thanks again for reminding me that I am worth every penny I earn and teaching me methods along with understanding the process of sales.

Kathy Dutton

"NO – it's just a two letter word. Approaching a prospect with the idea that you are going to see if they qualify to do business with your company is a wonderful concept! This certainly does eliminate the fear of them rejecting you. I think if I keep in mind the fact that the prospect is not rejecting me personally, and that them not wanting to do business with me is their loss not mine, it makes a person saying no more bearable. I have leaned that if I talk to enough people, someone will say yes."

Lisa Kirchner

6. What is the key to persistence?

Customers resist even the best ideas. The resistance starts with a negative feeling about the product, service or program. He or she hasn't looked into it yet. The immediate resistance is general. First of all, there's the risk. What if the idea doesn't pay off or the product doesn't perform?

Also, something new means change. And maybe the change will be uncomfortable. It will cause trouble, and who needs trouble?

All this makes the prospect feel that they don't want to hear about what you are trying to sell. Even if you get them to listen, their generalized resistance adds strength to the objection.

Your customer will be on the defensive before you even begin to sell. It is in a person's nature to fear making a change that will cost money. During a sales presentation, your customer will almost always respond negatively to your pricing. It is part of their strategy to get you to lower your price.

By knowing what to expect you avoid giving in without making a case for your product. Salespeople frequently make the mistake of offering discounts up front in order to head off a potentially negative discussion about price.

A sales manager I worked for insisted that I call on a certain account every week even though it seemed hopeless to ever sell them. On the very first call the customer tore my business card up in little pieces. The customer had a problem with a previous sales person. The sales person had left the company with a grudge and had left several things undone. This particular customer had several special orders for a banquet. The day the product was due for delivery the customer found out that the sales person had quit and never turned in the order. However, I followed orders and finally, after 37 weeks of calls, he gave in and bought something from me. If it had been up to me I never would have done it, however, the boss followed up and asked me every week if I made the call.

Have the necessary persistence to overcome their resistance and plan to outlast the competition. You have the knowledge of knowing you can turn them into a customer as long as you stay with it.

Do you have persistence? Take the test to see how much persistence you have. Ask yourself this one question - what is your biggest accomplishment and how long did it take to accomplish it? If you have a major accomplishment that took you over THREE YEARS - welcome to the club.

Persistence pays off. I have a couple of accounts that it took six months or longer to get a decent order. I continued to go see the accounts even though the orders I received were not worth my time. Both are among my better accounts now. In another stop, the customer disliked me because my company had fired my predecessor, whom the customer liked. After several months of verbal abuse and small orders, I offered to wash dishes for them on a day that some of their employees had failed to show up for work. They took me up on my offer and the next week they had a large order for me along with the comment that their other sales reps would not have washed dishes for them or kept coming by for so long.

Larry Edmondson

Persistence is the key to success in anything you do. Whether it be education, sales, or any other career avenue, you must be persistent in all that you do. Ever hear the saying "Easy come, Easy go"? There is a reason that business came to you easily. That is the same reason that business will leave you just as easily. You must be persistent and consistent in the growth and building of your business.

Scott Green

Persistence really does pay off in the long run - in large amounts! I think with persistence though, you really need to have it low key - like a social visit - rather than with the impression that you are irritating someone to try to get their business. Knowing how to be persistent to get the results you want to achieve and holding the customers interests at heart is the key.

Joanne Welsh

Persistence does pay off. When I was in sales with a large "strapping" company I had a customer that I called on every week and every week he told me he was happy with his current supplier and he was getting a better price on the strapping than I could give him. Every week I thanked him for his time and told him if the situation ever changed I would be there to help him. I called on him every week for four months and happen to catch him in a bad mood one day, his current supplier had let him down. Guess what, I got his order and all his future orders.

Vickie Reihl

I read somewhere that it can take up to 10-12 contacts before you close a sale. So with that in mind, I would say the best thing a sales professional can do to overcome resistance is to stay in contact with your potential client. My goal is for them to associate my name with the service/product I can help them with. To summarize... keeping yourself "Top of Mind" is key to building a lasting business relationship.

Becky Akins

Great lesson - persistence is the key to everything. Take a look at the greats in sports...Michael Jordan, basketball legend - cut from high school basketball;

Richard Petty, race car legend - not only more wins than any other racer; also more 2nds & 3rds;

Michelle Kwan, figure skater; not only more wins than any other skater, more 6.0's for perfect scores & still competing;

Phil Mickleson, finally a major win along with a great career.

In business you hear about it over & over again - Colonel Sanders, Sam Walton, Helen Keller, Thomas Edison - Oprah Winfrey, just to name a few.

Persistence is the one strength that is common in most all successful people. We have seen this happen over & over again in our industry (The staffing industry)

Heidi leaves cards, visit after visit after visit. Sometimes it is years before we ever get a call - but that persistence pays off.

I think that's why there is a lot of turn over in this industry - most people want that immediate gratification - can't wait - can't be persistent in reaching a goal, can't stay on task for years.

I also think this is an innate quality or ability that people are born with - not that it can't be learned or fine tuned - but for the most part you either have it or you don't.
Jean Smith

Here is one of the best stories of persistence on record. If you have never read the story of the Colonel - you are in for a treat...

Colonel Sanders (from the KFC website)

Colonel Harland Sanders, born September 9, 1890, actively began franchising his chicken business at the age of 65. Now, the KFC® business he started has grown to be one of the largest quick service food service systems in the world. And Colonel Sanders, a quick service restaurant pioneer, has become a symbol of entrepreneurial spirit.

More than a billion of the Colonel's "finger lickin' good" chicken dinners are served annually. And not just in North America. The Colonel's cooking is available in more than 80 countries and territories around the world.

When the Colonel was six, his father died. His mother was forced to go to work, and young Harland had to take care of his three-year-old brother and baby sister. This meant doing much of the family cooking. By the age of seven, he was a master of several regional dishes.

At age 10, he got his first job working on a nearby farm for $2 a month. When he was 12, his mother remarried and he left his home near Henryville, Ind., for a job on a farm in Greenwood, Ind. He held a series of jobs over the next few years, first as a 15-year-old streetcar conductor in New Albany, Ind., and then as a 16-year-old private, soldiering for six months in Cuba.

After that he was a railroad fireman, studied law by correspondence, practiced in justice of the peace courts, sold insurance, operated an Ohio River steamboat ferry, sold tires, and operated service stations. When he was 40, the Colonel began cooking for hungry travelers who stopped at his service station in Corbin, Ky. He didn't have a restaurant then, but served folks on his own dining table in the living quarters of his service station.

As more people started coming just for food, he moved across the street to a motel and restaurant that seated 142 people. Over the next nine years, he perfected his secret blend of 11 herbs and spices and the basic cooking technique that is still used today.

Sander's fame grew. Governor Ruby Laffoon made him a Kentucky Colonel in 1935 in recognition of his contributions to the state's cuisine. And in 1939, his establishment was first listed in Duncan Hines' "Adventures in Good Eating."

In the early 1950s a new interstate highway was planned to bypass the town of Corbin. Seeing an end to his business, the Colonel auctioned off his operations. After paying his bills, he was reduced to living on his $105 Social Security checks.

Confident of the quality of his fried chicken, the Colonel devoted himself to the chicken franchising business that he started in 1952. He traveled across the country by car from restaurant to restaurant, cooking batches of chicken for restaurant owners and their employees. If the reaction was favorable, he entered into a handshake agreement on a deal that stipulated a payment to him of a nickel for each chicken the restaurant sold. By 1964, Colonel Sanders had more than 600 franchised outlets for his chicken in the United States and Canada. That year, he sold his interest in the U.S. company for $2 million to a group of investors including John Y. Brown Jr., who later was governor of Kentucky from 1980 to 1984. The Colonel remained a public spokesman for the company. In 1976, an independent survey ranked the Colonel as the world's second most recognizable celebrity.

Under the new owners, Kentucky Fried Chicken Corporation grew rapidly. It went public on March 17, 1966, and was listed on the New York Stock Exchange on January 16, 1969. More than 3,500 franchised and company-owned restaurants were in worldwide operation when Heublein Inc. acquired KFC Corporation on July 8, 1971, for $285 million.

Kentucky Fried Chicken became a subsidiary of R.J. Reynolds Industries, Inc. (now RJR Nabisco, Inc.), when Heublein Inc. was acquired by Reynolds in 1982. KFC was acquired in October 1986 from RJR Nabisco, Inc. by PepsiCo, Inc., for approximately $840 million.

In January 1997, PepsiCo, Inc. announced the spin-off of its quick service restaurants -- KFC, Taco Bell and Pizza Hut -- into an independent restaurant company, Tricon Global Restaurants, Inc. In May 2002, the company announced it received shareholders' approval to change it's corporation name to Yum! Brands, Inc. The company, which owns A&W All-American Food Restaurants, KFC,

67

Long John Silvers, Pizza Hut and Taco Bell restaurants, is the world's largest restaurant company in terms of system units with nearly 32,500 in more than 100 countries and territories.

Until he was fatally stricken with leukemia in 1980 at the age of 90, the Colonel traveled 250,000 miles a year visiting the KFC restaurants around the world.

And it all began with a 65-year-old gentleman who used his $105 Social Security check to start a business.

7. How do you approach a new-account?

"I forgot they were coming!"

"I wonder how long this is going to take."

"My production supervisor is on vacation."

"My office manager called in sick this morning!"

"YIKES! Look at all the stuff they have with them!"

"There are two of them - they will probably never stop talking."

"This is going to take forever - I've got to do something - fast."

"I see they have a price book - good - I know how to get rid of them."

"I'll get a price quote on something and tell them they are way too high.""

If you are having the door slammed in your face before you even have a chance to say hello - you may be doing it wrong.

Let me explain.

Why do you go to the office before an appointment and gather a ton of brochures, fill your brief case with samples, get a complete product list, take your laptop, and ask someone else to go on the sales call with you?

Your first mistake is thinking that the potential customer is remotely interested in you or what you are selling. You mistakenly think that they want to read your brochures (they don't), listen to your sales pitch (they have a hundred other things that are more pressing) and ask questions about you and your company (they really don't care). You mistakenly think that you are showing the importance you put on the appointment because there are two of you.

When they agreed to the appointment - you caught them at a weak moment. I am sure you have heard of "buyers remorse". Let me introduce you to a new concept – "agreeing to an appointment remorse." As soon as they hang up the phone it starts - "Why did I agree to see that sales person?"

Agreeing to an appointment is like buying on a credit card - easy to make the purchase - hard to pay off. Something you said may have sparked a small interest during your initial phone conversation - that spark has long since gone out by the time you show up.

So the question is: Why do you bring all this stuff with you and why do you invite someone to go along? You might be thinking that the reason is to be prepared.

The answer is - you lack confidence. I know – that's tough to swallow – but it is the truth. Having all this stuff and bringing someone with you assures you that you will have something to talk about.

Here is a little known secret about selling. Your job is not to talk, but to listen - not to present, but to ask questions.

The first thing you have to do is lower the prospects defenses. You do this by going alone and not taking anything, or anybody, with you. No computer, no brochures, no prices, not even a brief case. This takes courage because most sales people are taught that their job is to "show and tell." When you walk into an account "unarmed" and simply ask permission to ask a few questions, there is very little pressure on the buyer and even less on you.

As a professional, you have to evaluate the account to see if it will be profitable for you to invest your time with them. You have to position yourself to be on the offensive rather than the defensive when making a new account call. If you don't have your price book and someone wants to put you on the defensive by asking for a price – simply say "I don't know" and continue to ask questions about their business.

The process of calling on an account without a lot of baggage is similar to a visit to the dentist or doctor - you would want a complete examination before getting an operation or having a tooth pulled.

The first time you try it you will feel "unprepared." That is a good sign - it means you are trying something new and at the brink of learning a new skill.

I would like to challenge you to make a few cold calls this week completely unarmed - not unprepared - just unarmed.

What are you going to talk about? You are not going to talk - you are going to ask questions.

What person in their right mind would say 'no' to a question like this: I am here to talk about YOU - do YOU mind if I ask YOU a few questions about YOUR business to see if I might be able to be of service to YOU and help YOU achieve YOUR goals?

Many times on a cold call I feel as if the customer is not hearing "Hi, I'm Crocker Smith...." but instead hearing "I need to borrow some money from you" or "may I have three or four hours of your time?". Developing the opening statement is hard to do and the customer is searching for their opening response as you speak to shut you down and get you out of their office.

Also, there are times when bringing a higher up makes the customer feel more important and lets them know that getting their business is important to you. But this is later in the sales process.

Crocker Smith

I like the challenge of approaching new businesses and clients.

My style isn't one of a pushy sales person so I approach the new business with confidence and questions. I like to find out how long they've been in business and what industry. I like building rapport by noticing things in the office that interest them but always bring it back to business. While they are telling me about themselves and their business I take mental notes. I usually ask if I could come spend more time with them at a later date. I ask if I could call them back to schedule a time once I have access to my calendar. I ask for a business card if one isn't offered and thank them for their time. Once I get back to the office I send them an e-mail thanking them for seeing me.

I usually call the next day to schedule a time to meet with them. Once the meeting is scheduled then it's time for me to uncover through SPIN questions the challenges the business may be having. (SPIN = Situational, Problematic, Implementation and Need pay off). In closing I ask if I could present them with some benefits that I uncovered that could benefit them.

Becky Akins

To make sure that the client is serious about this and about respecting your time, I always send an e-mailed invitation out of Outlook to drop in their calendar. I think this shows your level of seriousness about you're their time as well as your time. Usually have them commit a 2nd time via e-mail invite shows them you mean business.

I also believe in having a very well thought out approach to taking the client through our cycle.

"PPP", The purpose of this visit is..., The process of this visit will include, and hopefully the payoff to you is.... I think this helps with the 'appointment remorse' by telling them up front what your process and objectives are.

Kristan Wilson

"I agree! Confidence is a huge issue for many people. One suggestion I would like to offer is to NEVER go on a sales appointment to a company with out pulling them up on the net or calling the Chamber and finding out as much as you possibly can about them. This greatly relieves your stress in regard to what you may speak about and makes you look like you have cared enough to do your homework."

Lynn Mosely

"Going to a prospect with the idea that you are there to

listen to their needs takes the pressure off of them, but also off of the sales person. If I don't have a bunch of "stuff" to worry about presenting to someone, and am just there to talk to them, boy what a relief. I am guilty of feeling more confident when there a two of us making a sales call. I think this is because I don't like telling someone I don't know the answer to a question. Also, if there is something about our services that I have forgot to mention the other person can fill in the gaps. I had never thought about this being intimidating to the prospect. Definitely some good information to keep in mind."

Lisa Kirchner

"This is probably one of my favorite lessons so far. It's like watching a Joel Osteen program at home – this article was talking directly to me. I completely understand how fun and how different it is to bring someone along with you on a sales call. I call it a crutch. If I can't think of something to say – well, surely my partner can feel the voided tick tock of silence. "

"This article made me laugh – just yesterday I did finally catch a big client on the phone, after a four month chase, in a moment of weakness, and he finally agreed to meet me in person. AFTER several visits to the guard gate, written notes, emails, and a delivered Christmas card. I WONDER

IF HE NOW IS HAVING BUYERS REMORSE and asking –
WHY did I finally agree to let Angela in the gates and come
to my office? "

"The best advice of this session – to go in and listen and
propose this – I am here to talk about YOU and your
company to see what I can do for you to help you achieve
your goals."

Angela Brewer

Appointment Acceptance Remorse (AAR): Sounds like a
serious condition, and it can be. This usually occurs when
you accept an appointment with someone you don't THINK
you need to talk to, whether this is the case or not.

Side Effects: Sweating, nervousness, fear of lost time,
anxiety over pushy sales people.

The cure: The sales person can calm the fears by showing
the prospective client that they are not going to waste their
time. In fact, they are going to use this time to learn all a
bout the clients needs, and ways to help them make their
company run smoothly and become more profitable and
efficient.

Catalysts for aggravating this condition: You should always
avoid having extra sales-people "tag-along". This can make
the sufferer panic. Also, do not bring every pamphlet that

your company has ever published, this just means that you have more "stuff" to show the client, that they really aren't interested in, plus when you enter the office, you look as if you are moving in. The client booked the appointment with you, not your gadgets and gizmos. Leave your laptop in the car an dif they ask a question that requires it, tell them you have it in your car and you would be happy to retrieve it and show them.

For any other Sales questions, please consult Bob Oros, your sales MD.

Laura J. Czajka

Boy, oh boy, am I guilty of this one. I especially found the part about bringing someone with you, a trap I had recently been falling back into. I am a very motivated and independent person. I don't usually rely on anyone to make things happen for me. I am a make things happen for me and not to me kind of person.

But a few months ago, I found myself feeling not so confident and I became scared of making the final pitch by myself. I could make the initial contact, no problem, but when it came down to the final decision, agreement in hand, and price discussion, I was having cold feet about my ability to close the deal. So I was bringing that extra person with me. That person to help fill the void in conversation, that person whom I could look to if I got stuck...forgot my name...etc. Then I realized that, I am the person who will be handling this account and I don't want them to get the idea that "Bob" who accompanied me to the final meeting is really the person they need to speak to if there was a problem. I had to reassert myself as the one and only "the buck stops here" person with whom my clients needed to associate my company with. It's funny to me, that this was not an issue of laziness, but a maybe I wasn't as good as I thought I was feeling on my part. I think in sales as in any industry, you constantly have to reassess yourself and remember you will have ups and downs.

Kathie Luttrell

About the author Bob Oros

Regardless of whether you are reading one of his books or attending one of his programs, the most frequent comment is: "This guy has been there, he is one of us, I am going to use these strategies."

With over 2,000 speaking engagements in all 50 states and several international locations for manufacturers, distributors and associations, you can be sure you will get the results and information you are looking for. Prior to starting his speaking career, Bob served six years in the US Navy as a Communications Specialist and then worked his way from a street sales person to the position of National Sales Manager for a Fortune 200 company.

Bob has received awards for speaking, writing and marketing too numerous to mention.

Additional Topics by Bob Oros

Why Sales People Fail

The Power of Expectations

Add Value to Every Product

Never Make the First Offer

How to Justify Your Price

Lost in 60 Seconds

One Good Reason to Buy

Control a Buyer's Attitude

How to Create Demand

Smoke Screen Objections

Take the Risk Out of Sales

How Small Companies Get Big